ENTERING
into the
SECRETS
of
GOD

TAQUISHA WINSTON

ISBN 979-8-88616-732-0 (paperback)
ISBN 979-8-88616-733-7 (digital)

Christian Faith Publishing
832 Park Avenue
Meadville, PA 16335
www.christianfaithpublishing.com

Printed in the United States of America

Walking with God

Hello, my name is Taquisha Winston, and today we're going to be reading about how our walk with God gets hard at times. But through it all, we have to stand against whatever we're faced with to see the true victory of our trials.

As we take a walk through the valley of death, we must never forget how important it is to keep God as our right-hand man because anytime we step away from God, that gives the enemy time to attack. He can attack our lives through our minds, bodies, and soul. See, that's why God is so persistent with us about staying in the word. For one, it's to keep us equipped from the attack of the enemy; and two, it's to also teach us and guide us on how to overcome the trials and tribulations of life. When walking with God, you will see the good and the bad. He has never promised that we will have a trial-free life. If anyone is telling you that, close your ears immediately!

I encourage you to look in the mirror every day and tell yourself, "God will never leave me nor forsake me." This time in my life, He only tests us on what we've learned. Just keep going. Don't give up and don't look back on the past unless it's a lesson you're willing to learn from or to remind yourself of how far God has brought you in life. Don't let the way of life get you off track and off course of who God really is in your life.

Let's be like the lady in the Bible with the issue of blood for twelve years. The moment she had the opportunity to get close to Jesus, she took it. No matter how you're feeling or what you're facing, take every opportunity you have to get close to Jesus even if it's just calling His name. Yeah, she could have been upset and angry at Jesus, but she took what she knew about Him and trusted Him enough to walk through hundreds of people just to touch His garment. She knew that just by touching Him, she would be healed. She knew and thought, *If only I could just get a portion of Jesus, my problem would be solved.* I used that as an example to say that she didn't allow her situation to tell her how to feel about Jesus; she knew she had a right to be healed and went after Him. Sometimes you have to get out of your sickbed and call on the name of Jesus. We can't touch Him, but when we call His name, He shows up! During these times of hardship in the world is the best time to get in tune with the word of God. The attack upon us is not with flesh and blood but with spirits and principalities. Yes, we have to know the difference between God's doing and the enemy's attacks because too often we get those two mixed up. At times, God will send things our way to elevate us and move us on; and too many times, we write it off as the enemy and get discouraged and give up. But all the while, God is calling us to something great. That's why He tells us to have a spirit of discernment so that we can know Him and recognize what we're dealing with.

Being a Single Mom in Christ

Wow! Sometimes it's hard for me to believe that I'm a mom of four. I have three boys and one girl, and those babies are my world. Where do I start? Being a single mom is not a very easy job. We just make it look easy. As a mom, we are given extra strength from God. God has equipped us with extra endurance, patience, and strength; and the most important one is LOVE. God can take a single mom and use her for so many things. Before I get into it, I want to speak to my ladies real quick.

How God Can Use You and Your Scars

As a single mom, we have so many advantages in the kingdom of God. Hey, don't get me wrong. God honors unity and marriage just as much. Being a single mom gives me such a lead. I want to say, for starters, being a single mom, you don't have to wrestle with anyone else's opinion but your own. Yeah, we have children, and yes, we get distracted because we feel like, *Oh, if we just had help, things would be easier*. I'm speaking from my own experience. Yeah, I've had boyfriends, baby daddies, and even just male friends; and I have to say being single is the best way for me. While I was dating and being young and free as the world would say, it was not as so fulfilling as the world would describe. I grew up on Christ and loved Him from the bottom of my heart. It was something about the human flesh I couldn't resist. As I grew up, I did things I wasn't supposed to do and experienced things that were ungodly. Even in my worldly ways, God still chose me. The main thing that I have learned while walking with

God is patience, resting, and trusting in Him through it all. He never gave up on me even on days I felt like giving up. He still spoke His peace over me, and He ministered to me. I don't care what life brings your way, still trust in the Lord with all you have because your faith will never turn void.

What to Do when the Pressure Is upon You

This was my biggest test ever when it comes to trusting God. **"Will you still remain true to your faith when life suddenly takes a wrong turn?"** I remember growing up I was so in love and still is in love with God. See, as a child, I really didn't understand that even though God loves us, we still face challenges in life. I can remember that as a child and a teenager, God gave me just about everything I've asked for. I felt like a kid in the candy store who had the money to get whatever she/he wanted. Every prayer I've prayed was answered. Even in my wrongdoing, God still favored me, but it wasn't like I was just out doing bad things for no reason. I used to do things out of anger because growing up and being less fortunate was not fun for me at all. Even though God has and still is making a way for me and my children and family, there are still some desires that we, as women, want; and if we can't have them, oh, boy, what a mood we are in. See, my mom was a woman of God and still is. Anything we were lacking, God made sure He picked up the slack whether it was bills, clothes, and even shoes. He always gave us what was needed and sometimes wanted. And growing up with a single mom, sometimes we as children don't make healthy decisions. All we say is, "Mama, why this, and why we can't have that?" But a trying mother will say, "One day, my love." As I grew older, I began to seek God for my purpose in life, and that's when reality began to sink in. Before I get into the hardships I experienced and went through, let me break it down to you about God and the different stages of life. When you are a baby in Christ, that's the time in your life when God will treat you just like the baby you are; and for the record, there is no age on being a baby in Christ. I have met people who are in their thirties who are more advanced in God than someone who is fifty, and that's a twenty-year age difference. God will use those who are willing to be used. Our trials and tribulations are the very things God uses to strengthen us and build our character in Him. You have to be careful transitioning from a baby to a teenager and to an adult because you will lose not only your faith but also yourself. When you hit a point in your life where God says, "Okay, it's time to grow up now," also the majority of God is trying to get us to the place to receive our blessing and to walk into our divine purpose. When you pray and ask God for better things in life, just remember that you can't stay in the same place you were in as a child. Those easy results become a little tougher, and prayers take a little longer to get answered. At that point, it's God saying, "Okay, now that it's not so easy, do you trust me to do what you've asked me for" Do you think you're ready for the things you have asked God for until He starts plucking, pruning, shaping, and molding you into the person He has predestined you to be? And that goes back to me saying you have to be careful not to lose yourself.

Have you ever cried out to God, and it feels like He's not listening? I believe we all have been there, which is a part of our metamorphosis stage in becoming who we are going to be and what purpose God has spoken over our lives, which was spoken over us at birth. When God takes us through the different stages of life, which means leveling us up in Him, we seem to want to step back from that point in our life; but really, that's the place where God molds us and builds us. Getting us to our destiny isn't a walk in the park for God either. Some of us shut down so quickly, and so often on that journey where it delays us, God is processing us because God works on faith. He moves according to what we believe and how we believe. Don't delay yourself. Let God take you to your promised land. Don't get stuck in the wilderness, complaining and missing out on the blessings God has for you on the way to your destiny. We sometimes miss out on the in-between blessings because we're focused on the destiny blessing. Maybe God wants to add more to you and your name, but you're too busy complaining and missing out on the things He's teaching you while you're on your way. **Never get caught up in the now and miss out on your tomorrow**. Do you know that every time you complain is a day God says, "Hold up. You stopped trusting. Get back on track." And if you continue, He pauses and sends something your way to get your attention—a word, a dream, or even a vision—something that enlightens your spirit to keep going. The secret to getting to where you are going on time is obedience and patience. Yeah, sometimes there's a delay so make sure everything and everyone is in the right place. Don't get stuck complaining. Don't allow yourself to stay in one place too long because God isn't moving on your time or doing it your way. Stop expecting God to be a magician because He's not. He grants prayers, not wishes, because prayers take time, and wishes take seconds. One is always going to outlast the other. Prayer is power and divine connection with God; it's his telephone line for us. **My point is that don't allow your life trials and tribulations take you away from the love and promises God has spoken over you and your children or future children.**

My Life and the Hardships I Dealt with on My Journey

I would like to start by saying I've had my share of heartaches, and I've had my share of joy; but through it all, I survived! As I mentioned before, growing up wasn't all cupcakes and rainbows; but with a praying mother, things didn't seem so bad until you get older enough to understand her prayers and struggles in life. It wasn't until I had my second child (well, they were twins) that God really began to deal with me. He started downloading things into my spirit, giving me ideas and just pouring them into me at a young age when I birthed my twins at nineteen. And that's when God spoke these words to me, "Hey! It's time to grow up now. I have things for you to do, and you have little time to get it together." The moment I received the things God told me and gave Him my yes, that's when my life took a turn toward maturity. During my pregnancy, there were a few complications where they didn't think my babies were going to be healthy. They were giving me all these speeches about the different possibilities and outcomes, but I stood by God's word and kept my faith. My babies were born nine minutes apart, both healthy five-pound babies. At thirty-five weeks, God showed up for me in that delivery room, which I didn't think I was going to make it at all because the anesthesia wore off while I was pushing. So I felt everything you could possibly feel, almost closing my legs on my baby. I was so tired. I needed oxygen. And at that moment, I became a mother of three, and I knew in my mind it was time to get it together. Thank God for my mother. She was there every step of the way as much as she could be. And even then, God was dealing with me on my own. I had to start learning to hear His voice for myself and learning discernment all while being a mother of three. I did what I've seen my mom do as a mother.

These feelings became uncomfortable inside me. Sometimes I couldn't sleep or even eat because there was something going on inside me that's changing. I would get frustrated a lot at times because I didn't understand what was going on. I would cry and pray and even fast. Time went by with no answer, but I kept crying and asking God, "Why I am feeling like this? What are you trying to tell me?" Still, there was no answer. This is what I meant when I said don't lose yourself while transitioning from that baby stage. During my transition, I was angry, frustrated, and confused because there was a change in my spirit I didn't understand. It was as if the places I was dwelling in weren't satisfying me anymore. I couldn't sit around certain friends, or I couldn't be in certain relationships. I used to get angry and ask why people are ignoring me and why no one calls me as much as they used to. I was at a point I felt lonely and bored. My mom used to say, "You got three kids. Go play with them." I knew she meant no harm, but at the time, I didn't find it funny. I remember everywhere I went a guy or three would try to talk to me or take me out and treat me to dinner or shopping. It's like in a blink of an eye, it all changed. I felt like I was ugly. I said to the Lord, "What's wrong with me?" and He said, "I am taking you to another level, and all that is old must leave and can't stay even your way of thinking!" And in that moment, I understood all the anger and frustration. When you don't understand what's going on with you or why you're feeling a certain way it does anger you and makes you feel funny, just know when you begin feeling like that, God is pruning you and taking you to a higher level in Him. And that can't be anymore. Them old friends, old relationships, and old ways can't go to the new place you've been desiring for; and He's really looking out for your better interest because He knows who is for you and who is against you. Even though at the time we might not want to, that's the time in your life where you must shout to the heavens knowing your backstabbers can't go to the next level with you.

Losing Sight of God in an Unhealthy Relationship

Ladies, I want to talk to you on this one. Ladies, we are natural-born lovers; and in our nature, whatever we see broken, we try and fix it. And that is where a lot of us women go wrong in relationships and even friendships. We are like the handymen ready to go to work and fix things. Well, see, God has equipped us women with super strength and the power of unconditional love. You see, when things fail and fall right before our feet, it hurts us the most because we put our all into it. Really, we sometimes forget about ourselves in the process. That's why we take heartbreak so hard to the heart. When a woman is upset and hurt, she will try to make you feel the same pain you made her feel even if it hurts her in the process. Being a woman, especially a woman of God, we tend to play God, not on purpose, not intentionally, but we do. Being there for others, canceling your plans to make sure the family is in order, paying for things, and making it easy on our men, making sure they're comfortable, trying to make the family get along, losing sleep over who said this about you, trying to force an answer from God to see which way to go, and even God is being quiet. What do you do as a woman when all odds are against you? What do you do? My answer to that is REST. We can be so busy with others that we lose sight of God. Ladies, we are running, running, running, and running to where we have no time to hear and see what the Father is telling us. We as women will run until we have no more fuel left in us. Even for those we know who don't care for us, our heart is willing to go to the end of the earth for the person or thing we love. But REST, honey, and hear what God is saying to you! How are you going to get that business plan you've been asking God for? Working full time, partying with friends, taking on your children, being a counselor, or a girlfriend playing wifey trying to prove your worth to be married, that alone can wear you out trying to prove a point to someone who's not acknowledging it. Don't lose sight of God because you're so busy trying to be a superwoman to everyone else except for yourself. Sit down, take ten or fifteen minutes out of your day. Talk to God, pray, write your business plan out, meditate, get the kids on a schedule, and allow someone to help you except help get out of the independent mentality and accept it because you need it. Even if you have to find extra activities for the kids to do a program for three or four hours, that's extra time you have to REST; and at night, while they're sleeping, put on worship music. Soft, peaceful music makes them feel peaceful and relaxed and makes them listen to Bible stories. I say that to say don't lose yourself and be a mom. I know children will be children, but as a mother, you need rest too. Tell yourself every day, **"I am who God has called me to be. I am a child of the Most High. I am victorious. I am who God says I am!"**

How Not to Settled in Unequally Yoked Relationships

This topic is very important, and I see this in so many relationships—being unequally yoked with a person. If you're ever wondering why things in the relationship don't work out, well I'm going to break a few of those reasons down. The number one reason for an unhealthy relationship is staying connected with someone who God already told you and showed you was not the right one for you. But love can make you make those mistakes time after time after time. Number two is staying connected with someone because they help you financially but make you unhappy spiritually. Number three, staying only with someone because of flesh desires. These are the top three relationships that don't last or become unhealthy. These are the top three reasons for a failed marriage, friendship, or just someone you're connected to. You can also be unequally yoked in friendships as well. When God was dealing with me about being unequally yoked with a person, He was referring to friendship.

When you are going to this new level in Christ, you can sometimes feel like a deer in headlights. Even though we have entered into that new elevated, new level, it can still feel like we're in the same place. That's because we're not seeing anything change or feeling the change, so when you doubt, you're denying yourself of operating on the new level, an elevated level in Christ.

There will be times when God will give you a word of encouragement. Yeah, you will be happy, but how long will you keep that smile before you say, "Okay, God. How long before I can see those things that you have promised me?" And that's when you get anxious here and there, anticipating and worrying about something that's going to happen but in God's time, not yours. You will find yourself in a restless situation if you don't settle down and trust God. We have to realize that when God is speaking things to us, it may sometimes happen at a later time, which we as humans get confused about. Sometimes God will speak a word, and it won't happen until five or ten years later. Sometimes it takes months, but it will happen. If you don't watch it, you will allow the enemy to sneak in and use that very thing to attack you and take your mind off of God. How do I know? It's because I have experienced it firsthand. I remember God was speaking these very powerful words and telling me who I was and who I was going to become, and at that moment, I realized God had called me to do great things. But if anybody would have told me that nine years later I would still be waiting, I wouldn't have pushed through with the things that God had taken me through. Yeah, I have cried many days and couldn't eat or sleep because it was allowing my impatience to see the promises come to pass. Sometimes God will step in and say, "Hey, don't miss what I have given you on the way to your destiny. Don't despise the wait because, in the wait, I'm teaching you and molding you!" One thing I really want you to get out of this is not to despise the wait because, in the wait, there are hidden treasures of God. Trust me. He has given me many, and this book is one of them.

How to Enter into the Rest of God

Entering into God's rest is one of the hardest things to do when you're waiting on a miracle, His promises, or even just simply waiting for a solution to your problem. I think we wrestle with rest so much because we don't know the end result of the problem we face. Yeah, we hear all the time to just trust God and that He will fix it. Rest, God got it. What do you do when those words don't work for you, and you're still trying to get an answer out from God. What do you do? Well, you rest. One thing about God that I know is that He CANNOT work on your behalf if you're not resting. What I mean by resting is to relax your mind, breathe, and take a break from worrying about those things you can't control. What has worrying and being all upset gotten you besides a trip to the doctor and to your local pharmacy to get a Tylenol? I know, I've been there.

If God has said it, then it's done; and even in our frustration, He will speak! He will always speak a peace that passes all understanding, but it's up to you if you take the word and eat it. What I mean by eating the word is to enjoy it. Let your spirit enjoy that meal of words God has just spoken into you. When you go to a restaurant and you eat, what do you do? Enjoy it, right? So that's how you do the word of God. When you read it or even hear it, enjoy it to the fullest because hearing from God is a blessing. It's an even bigger blessing to be called by Him as well. Don't let the enemy take what God has given you and turn it around and make you miserable or unhappy because he will do it if you let him. He knows that if you lack rest, you can't function right. Your mind will be uneasy, and you won't be able to hear what the Lord is trying to tell you because you're tired. I don't care if you have to put your phone on DND (do not disturb). Make time for God. Don't count Him out of your life because He doesn't forget to wake you up, put food on your table, and provide you with finances to put a roof over your head; just don't forget about God.

Come to God with a sound mind and a restful spirit so that the answer you are looking for can be given. God will purposely be quiet just to see if we will still trust Him even if He doesn't answer us. And sometimes, the test of quietness can be one of the hardest tests because you want to know, "What's next, God? And where am I going?" And if you're not careful, the enemy will slip in and play with your mind and make it seem like God, but the whole time it's not. That's why He tells us to take advantage of the waiting process. What can you learn while you're waiting to see those things He promised come to pass? When you take those things, you have learned and apply them to your everyday life. You will be grateful for the waiting process because now you're wiser and a little more mature than when you first started out. Just wait upon the Lord, and He will renew your strength and restore your joy!

How to Not Lose Your Soul while Chasing Your Desires

Desires, desires, desires. This can be a good thing, and it can be a bad thing. The word *desire* is the core reason why people do the things they do. When you hear an older person who has been working all their life say, "I had to work to get what I want, and, I'm going to keep going until I get to that point, and then I'll retire." Or you will hear a young person who's been in poverty all his life say, "I've got to get it by any means. I'm tired of being broke." Those are some of the mindsets we have to fulfill the desires of our hearts. A broke man will do whatever he has to do because he desires to live a better life, and an older person will work all his life because he desires to retire at one point and never have to worry about going without. And sometimes, we will lose ourselves in doing it to the point where we stop trusting God and spending time with Him because we're so busy trying to satisfy the flesh and deny the soul. Jesus said, "Let any man deny himself, pick up his cross and follow me." That means that when you begin to follow Jesus, your fleshly desires have to go. You must lay down the old you and allow God to renew you into the image of Jesus."

We have treated God like He is some kind of magician or genie, which he is not. You don't snap your fingers or rub a bottle, and He pops out and grants those wishes. He answers prayers and tears, not commands, when you want it and how you want it. As a matter of fact, He takes His time when it comes to giving you those things because He has to take the old you and remold you and change your mind so you can operate on that new level, and that doesn't happen overnight. I always use the reference, "The longer the wine sits, the better it tastes. The more potent, the more it costs." Remember that.

Just know that God is not a God of half stepping, and He loves us so much that He will give us an unexpected blessing, something that will make us smile and happy while waiting. And it might be something that you have been wanting for a while and forgotten about it, but God hasn't. Never underestimate the process of waiting because the wait is a place of gaining knowledge, wisdom, increase, and ideas. God has given me so many ideas along the way, but He had to get me to the place in my life where I can receive them and be joyful about them.

Once you get to a place in your life where you can see the beauty of God in every aspect of your life, then you begin to be thankful for the wait because now you say, "Lord, if you would have given it to me in the place I was in, I would have lost it all, but because of your wisdom and omniscience, you've seen the things I couldn't see." I say these words to myself all the time. "Father, you saw my enemies when I couldn't. You saw who was against me and who was for me. You knew who would betray me and use me. You knew those who were out to destroy me, yet you kept me. So I thank you for being God and looking out for me when I couldn't look out for myself." So be grateful for the wait. It's a blessing to wait a little longer. The longer the wait, the bigger the blessing. The bigger the blessing, the longer you get to keep it. Remember that. Always give thanks unto the Lord in all your ways in doing things. This means that whatever you do, do it unto the Lord Jesus Christ because He paid the ultimate price and paid the way for us all to have the privileges we have now. Without the blood of Jesus, you're lost and roaming this world uncovered. Wherever you are in life right now, enjoy the wonders of it because not many live to see today.

How to Push through when You're Tired

I saved the best for the last—**pushing through when you're tired**. In today's society, being tired is the most common thing. It feels like in these recent times and days, we are facing so much difficulty. There has been some good and some bad, and too many are feeling like the bad has outweighed the good. Some people are reaping what they sowed, and many are reaping the harvest of their seed. And during this time, God is repaying back what you put out in these past years. I remember God telling me, "This is the season of reaping. What you have sown, whether it's good or bad, you will get what you have planted in the earth or in my kingdom."

Allow yourself to enter into the hands of God. Allow Him to shelter you and protect you. Allow Him to cover you and show you. *Allow* is the key word of this paragraph. Because God will not force Himself onto us. He gives us our own free will to choose, and once you allow God to enter into your life and fix the thing you've been stressing about, He will begin to remove those things. Sometimes those things are the closest people to us like friends, lovers, family, and even our own parents. They can be our downfall. I say that because when your own parents can't see the vision or can't seem to support you, that is what takes effect on you the most. And trying to prove to someone who you are and what God has given you can make you very drained and tired. Stop letting people drain you and pull from you. Don't allow anyone else to approve of you but God.

Enter into the rest of God because without Him, you are nothing but an empty soul, searching for something and someone who can fill that void. Do not allow yourself to get so wrapped up in someone else's life that it takes from yours. If you're a person who prays for people, and God speaks to you, don't force them to listen. Just say what you have to say and move on. Quit allowing people to put their burdens on you. You're only one person. You're not God, so don't let anyone make you their God or crunch because I guarantee you, life will be like carrying two times the load. And sometimes we put more on ourselves than what we can bear, not God. And we look to God like it's His fault, and He's saying to you, "I didn't tell you to take on that person. I just said pray for them and tell them what I said. I never told you to do my job because you are not qualified for my job. You are tired because you're trying to be me to everyone else, and you're not even letting me be me to you. Pick up your own cross and follow me. Everyone is responsible for their own actions. If you allow others to lean on you, then who will be there for you to lean on? Stop doing my job and only do the job I have assigned to you. If there's anything else I need from you, I will come to you. But other than that, rest in me and on me. Give me all your burdens. Carry only what I have given you, nothing more or nothing less. Whether you know it or not, they're taking you away from me. You're so tired that you can't do what I have for you to do. Step back and rest. REST, REST, REST because your rest is important." If the devil can keep you up and going, then he will. He knows rest is the way of focusing and hearing from God, but a cluttered and confused mind and a tired soul have nothing to offer to God. Let him renew you, strengthen you, help you save you, and mold you. Don't let the enemy snatch you away from God in any way at all. Even in marriage, give yourself some personal time with God. Yeah, He honors marriage and unity, but there will also be a time He has each of you to do something different. But He will allow you to be there to help one another. Don't get offended. Don't get upset and start an argument. YES, there will be times He will have each of you alone and on different assignments. Pray and get an understanding. Respect one another and obey God's word. Let Jesus teach you and the Holy Spirit guide you. Let

God be your refuge and soar like an eagle. When it comes to His direction, just flow in it like a fish flow in the water. Just glide in it like a parachute glides you to a landing. Sit and meditate more, dissect the word, be in tune with His word, and don't be so easily shaken by the snares of the enemy.

Rest because you matter to the world. You are important to us, so keep going. You fit into God's plan somewhere. You matter I know you do because God doesn't make any junk or trash. He can turn our trash ways into the treasures of His kingdom. I don't care what anybody says. You matter in the eye of the beholder who is God. Jehovah Jireh, Jehovah-Nissi, Jehovah-Rapha, and El-Shaddai are just a few names of God. But never forget that even if you have to look at yourself in the mirror every day and tell yourself, "Hey, I matter to God and myself!"

Becoming One with the Holy Spirit

Being in covenant with the Holy Spirit is a beautiful thing. When God created the Holy Spirit, He thought of unity, He thought of guidance, and He thought of us because he knew we would need spiritual intimacy. It's not only being in tune with the Holy Spirit, but it's also the gifts that come along with the Holy Spirit. My favorite gift is speaking in tongues. Oh, what a beautiful language that only God can understand. The gift of tongues is the Holy Spirit pulling out the things of your heart that you can't even speak or pray. He takes us to God through the spiritual realm and sits us before the throne and speaks on our behalf in a heavenly language.

That's why God is so big on relationships. When having a relationship, you trust you have recognition. No one can come and tell you anything about someone you know. Because you have a relationship with them, you have spent enough time with that person to know their ways. And that's how God wants us to be with the Holy Spirit—to get to know Him and let Him in. Accept the gift of the Holy Spirit. One day, you're going to need Him. Let the Holy Spirit give you the gift of discernment. We need to know when there is a snake in the grass, or is it the Spirit of God leading us. Become one with the Spirit of God, which is the access to it all. Jesus paid the way for us all that's why God gives us the Bible and the prophets and the pastors to help us get to the point in our life, where He has destined us to be.

Become one with God. Become one with the Holy Spirit! Become one with Jesus. Don't let your life perish away and not be connected to the power source. God is our power source. We should thrive off of Him, live off of him, allow Him to enter into your hearts today, and pick and pluck those things that are destroying you, hurting you. Forgive those who have done you evil. I know it might be hard but forgive for yourself, not for them. They're going on with their life. You should go on with yours! Let God heal you and allow Jesus to hold you and let the Holy Spirit guide you no matter what you will need at one point in your life.

Flow is the key word of this book. Why I say *flow* is because when you flow with something, you're in rhythm. You're in sync with it, in tune. Be in tune with the word of God. Stay focused and stay equipped with the word of wisdom and let us say AMEN!

Walking with Dominion

Walking with dominion means walking like you have it, like you already own it. Walking with dominion also means walking with the authority God has given you. Claim what's yours. Claim it with **boldness. Don't let the devil take away your boldness!** Stand firm in the Lord, so He can renew you and purify you in the mighty name of Jesus.

A quick prayer of boldness, **"Lord I come to you with boldness in my heart and firmness with my feet. I take dominion over all things you have given me. I call out (anything you're claiming dominion over) peace and prosperity over my children and an increase in my finances. I take back all those things the enemy has stolen from me. The theft is caught, and he must return what is stolen from me. I command the heaven of the host to go and take those things that belong to me and restore them to me in** THE MIGHTY NAME **of** JESUS, AMEN!**"**

Don't ever forget to come boldly before God in what you want. Don't be scared to come to God as a child would come to their father for something. Stop being so easily shaken and broken. It's okay to cry, but when you do, wipe your eyes. Do your hair shower and smile. Ladies, cook, shop online, get your hair done, feel life again. Fellas, go get a haircut, take your wife on a date, watch sports, go out with the guys, and enjoy life

again. Don't let stress rob you of life. You only have one life, enjoy it.

I wouldn't tell you anything I haven't experienced
myself. Love you, and I hope you received and
enjoyed my message today with the love of God.
Have a wonderful and blessed filled day!

—Taquisha Winston

About the Author

Entering into the secrets of God is a book of inspiration. When Taquisha Winston began writing the book, she wrote from her own personal experiences with God. Taquisha is a mother of four and a woman of many ideas within her. She takes her life one day at a time by walking with God and allowing Him to guide her and teach her how to become a woman that He desires her to be. Life was not always easy for her. There have been ups and downs, twists and turns, but through it all, she made it. Her tears and frustration are what made her the woman she is today. This book is a book written from the heart from which God Himself dwells within. While writing this book, she thought about those who might need some encouragement on how to get close to God and trust Him through all circumstances of life. She is a walking testimony, and she hopes this book will inspire you to keep pushing and to never give up on God in Jesus's name, amen!